AT WHAT JAZZ CLUB DID THE ROLLING STONES MAKE THEIR DEBUT?

WHAT IS MICK JAGGER'S REAL FIRST NAME?

WHICH MEMBER OF THE BEATLES APPEARED WITH THE ROLLING STONES ON "ROCK 'N' ROLL CIRCUS"?

WHO WAS "UNCLE GENE" ON THE STONES' RECORDING "NOW I'VE GOT A WITNESS (LIKE UNCLE PHIL AND UNCLE GENE)"?

(Answers Below)

These are just a few of the brainteasers you'll find in this collection of quizzes on the earliest, the latest, and the greatest happenings in the careers of the Stones, one of the all-time top rock groups in the world. So tune your mind into the right beat, and see if you know all the answers to the puzzlers in

THE ROLLING STONES TRIVIA QUIZ BOOK

The Marquee

Michael

John Lennon

Gene Pitney

THE ROLLING STONES TRIVIA QUIZ BOOK

by

Helen Rosenbaum

A SIGNET BOOK
NEW AMERICAN LIBRARY
TIMES MIRROR

PUBLISHED BY
THE NEW AMERICAN LIBRARY
OF CANADA LIMITED

First Signet Printing May 1979
1 2 3 4 5 6 7 8 9

SIGNET TRADEMARK REG. U.S. PAT. OFF. AND FOREIGN COUNTRIES
REGISTERED TRADEMARK — MARCA REGISTRADA
HECHO EN WINNIPEG, CANADA

SIGNET, SIGNET CLASSICS, MENTOR, PLUME and MERIDIAN BOOKS are published in Canada by The New American Library of Canada Limited, Scarborough, Ontario

PRINTED IN CANADA
COVER PRINTED IN U.S.A.

For Professor I. Harold Kellar,
who is not part of The Stone Age.
He would rather swing and sway
to the music of Sammy Kaye.

QUESTIONS

1. PREHISTORIC ROLLING STONES

1. Mick Jagger's first group while still in school was called Little Boy ——— and the Blue Boys.

2. In addition to Mick, members of the Blue Boys included Keith Richard and Dick ———.

3. Dick later became a member of the ——— Things.

4. Identify the four tracks on the tape of the Blue Boys that Mick Jagger sent to Alexis Korner.

5. The leader and driving force behind the Rolling Stones in the early days was not Jagger but rather what other original group member?

6. Charlie Watts was once a member of Blues by ——.

7. He joined the Stones, replacing drummer Tony ——.

8. Bill Wyman auditioned for the Rolling Stones at the ——— Arms. He was accepted into the group partly because he had a large ———.

9. In 1962, Mick Jagger, Keith Richard, and Brian Jones shared a flat in ——— Grove, Chelsea.

10. In an attempt to find more work, the Rolling Stones joined the National ——— Federation.

2. ALEXIS KORNER: SOUL & INSPIRATION

1. Alexis Korner began his career as a member of the ——— Barber Band. Name the singing star Barber was once married to.

2. In 1961, Alexis formed Blues ———.

3. Mick Jagger and Keith Richard first heard Alexis and his group at the ——— Club in London.

4. Name the two musicians in Alexis Korner's blues band who later became members of the Rolling Stones.

5. Identify the vocalist Mick heard with Alexis' blues group. This vocalist later became the lead singer with ——— Mann.

6. In what year did Mick Jagger join Alexis Korner's group as vocalist?

7. Every Thursday, Mick sang with Alexis' group at the ——— Jazz Club in London.

8. Name the British music newspaper that carried the first notice of Mick joining Alexis' group.

9. Alexis hired drummer ——— Baker to replace the drummer who later joined the Rolling Stones. In later years, Baker distinguished himself as a member of which two supergroups with Eric Clapton?

10. Alexis Korner has been called "Father of the white ——— blues."

3. EARLY STONE AGE

1. The Rolling Stones made their debut at what jazz club?

2. Give the exact date of this original appearance.

3. Who was the manager of this jazz club?

4. Name the first English newspaper to review the Rolling Stones. What was the date of the article?

5. ——— Records in England signed the Stones, having once turned down the Beatles.

6. Dick ——— was the record-company executive who rejected the Beatles and gave the Stones a contract.

7. ——— Records distributed the Stones' releases in America for many years.

8. Give the English release date of the Stones' first single, "Come On."

9. What is the name of the British TV show the group appeared on to promote the record?

10. Name the Rolling Stones' first American album. Give the month and year of its release.

4. ANDREW OLDHAM: MILLION-DOLLAR HYPE

1. What is Andrew Oldham's middle name?

2. Give the two stage names Andrew used in his brief career as a singer.

3. Andrew was working for talent agent Eric ——— when they became co-managers of the Rolling Stones.

4. Identify the English group whose publicity Andrew briefly handled before adding to the Stones' great unwashed image.

5. Andrew and Eric signed the Rolling Stones to a management contract in 1963 after hearing them perform at the Station Hotel's ——— Club in Richmond.

6. Giorgio ———, who was running this club at the Station Hotel, had only a verbal agreement to manage the Stones at the time.

7. Eric and Andrew formed ——— Sound, an independent record label to control all aspects of the Rolling Stones' releases.

8. Name both sides of the Rolling Stones' first single produced by Andrew.

9. This first record was initially cut at ——— Sound Studios on May 10, 1963. The recording engineer at the session was Roger ———.

10. What is the title of the song Andrew later co-wrote with Keith Richard?

5. STONE COUNTDOWN

Fill in the blanks using Rolling Stone arithmetic to complete the following song, EP, and album titles.

1. "——— More Try"
2. "Route ———"
3. "———th Nervous Breakdown"
4. "Flight ———"
5. "——— Light-Years from Home"
6. "——— South Michigan Avenue"
7. "——— Man"
8. "——— by Five"
9. "12× ———"
10. "——— Years Ago"

6. MICK JAGGER: NO BOY SCOUT

1. What is Mick's real first name?
2. Indicate his middle name.
3. Give Mick's date of birth.
4. What is his sun sign?
5. Mick once listed his stage name as Vince ———.
6. Give the first names of Mick's mother and father.
7. His father teaches ——— education.
8. What color are Mick's eyes?
9. Mick attended ——— County Primary School with what other future member of the Rolling Stones?
10. Early in his career, Mick dated model Jean Shrimpton's sister ———.

7. THE ROLLING STONES ZOO

Fill in the blanks, identifying the appropriate animals, insects, and assorted wildlife. You will be completing the titles of Stones' recordings and one as-yet unreleased track of a soul classic. Also included here: a tune from a Bill Wyman solo album.

1. "Little Red ———"
2. "I'm a ——— for You, Baby"
3. "The ——— and the Fly"
4. "——— Grip Glue"
5. "Walking the ———"
6. "——— of Burden"
7. "Wild ———"
8. "I'm a King ———"
9. "Stray ——— Blues"
10. "——— Man"

8. BRIAN: BLONDES DON'T ALWAYS HAVE MORE FUN

1. His full name was ——— Brian Hopkin-Jones.
2. Brian was born in the English suburb of ———, Gloucestershire.
3. Give the date of Brian's birth.
4. What is his sun sign?
5. Give Brian's most popular nickname.
6. Very early in his career, Brian was a member of a local band known as the ———.
7. What are the first names of Brian's mother and father?
8. His sister's first name is ———.
9. Brian's former girlfriend Linda Lawrence later married Scottish-born folksinger/songwriter ——— Leitch, better known by his first name.
10. Rolling Stones Records released the album, "Brian Jones Presents the Pipes of Pan at ———." This album featured the performance of native musicians recorded in what country?

9. STONES (IN PARENTHESES)

Match the titles of the following songs—recorded and mostly written by the Rolling Stones—to their subtitles in parentheses. Also included here is the title of a Stones album.

1. "Oh Baby"	a. (Mona)
2. "Sing This All Together"	b. (Running Away with Me)
3. "Doo Doo Doo Doo Doo"	c. (Like Uncle Phil and Uncle Gene)
4. "Tell Me"	d. (Heartbreaker)
5. "Just My Imagination"	e. (We Got a Good Thing Going)
6. "Satisfaction"	f. (Walkin' Thru the)
7. "I Need You, Baby"	g. (You're Coming Back)
8. "More Hot Rocks"	h. (See What Happens)
9. "Now I've Got a Witness"	i. (I Can't Get No)
10. "Sleepy City"	j. (Big Hits & Fazed Cookies)

10. KEITH & HIS TEETH

1. What is the full last name of Keith Richard?

2. Give Keith's date of birth.

3. What is his sun sign?

4. Keith attended ——— Art School.

5. He once used the stage name ——— Masters.

6. Anita Pallenberg left which other member of the Rolling Stones for Keith?

7. What is the first name of Anita's and Keith's son born in 1969.

8. Their daughter has the same first name as the Rolling Stones hit single, "———."

9. After many rumors, Keith admitted he was having his ——— fixed.

10. The lyrics of a Nils Lofgrin recording warned, "Keith, Don't Go to ———."

11. STONES' HOT WAX WOMEN

The Rolling Stones sang of the following women. Answer true or false after each name including one bootleg cut by the group. And one track from a solo album by Ron Wood.

1. "Ana"
2. "Soulful Sybil"
3. "Sherry"
4. "Angie"
5. "Jennifer"
6. "Carol"
7. "Shirley"
8. "Connie"
9. "Beautiful Delilah"
10. "Donna"

12. IS BILL OVER THE HILL?

1. Bill Wyman's real name is William ———.

2. The oldest Stone: Although some publications list the year of his birth as 1941, Bill was born on October 24, ———.

3. What is his sun sign?

4. Bill has ——— sisters and brothers.

5. Identify the branch of the British Armed Forces in which Bill served for two years.

6. What is the first name of the woman Bill married in 1959 and later divorced?

7. Give the first name of Bill's son from this marriage.

8. Bill has been linked with ——— Lundström.

9. Before joining the Rolling Stones, Bill formed his own group, the ———.

10. What are the titles of Bill's two solo albums?

13. THE STONES & "I"

Me, Myself and I: Fill in the blanks, completing the titles of those songs performed and mostly written by the Stones plus title of a cut from one of Bill Wyman's solo albums and releases from both of former Stone Ron Wood's solo albums.

1. "I Can't Stand the ———"
2. "I Can't Be ———"
3. "(I Can't Get No) ———"
4. "I Can Say She's ———"
5. "I Can Feel the ———"
6. "I Got a ———"
7. "I Got Lost When I ——— You"
8. "I Am ———"
9. "I Wanna Get Me a ———"
10. "I Don't Know ———"

14. CHARLIE: WATTS WHAT

1. What is Charlie's middle name?

2. Give his date of birth.

3. Identify the drummer's sun sign.

4. He attended ——— Art School.

5. In the beginning, Charlie combined his musical career with a full-time job at the ——— and Gray Advertising Agency.

6. What is the first name of the woman Charlie married in 1964?

7. Charlie and his wife are the parents of a daughter named ———, born in 1968.

8. Identify the title of the book Charlie wrote and illustrated about jazz-great Charlie Parker.
9. "The ——— Band" album was produced by Charlie Watts.

10. He is a former president of the North Wales ——— Society, pointing up his diversified interests.

15. DAY, NIGHT & IN-BETWEEN TIME

Fill in the blanks, completing the titles of these timeless tunes, recorded and mostly written by the Stones.

1. "——— and Every Day of the Year"
2. "The ——— Time"
3. "Through the ——— Nights"
4. "Good Times, ——— Times"
5. "Yesterday's ———"
6. "Time Is on My ———"
7. "Midnight ———"
8. "——— Time"
9. "Let's ——— the Night Together"
10. "——— of Time"

16. IAN STEWART: STONE ANONYMOUS

1. What is Ian Stewart's nickname?

2. The press sometimes refers to Ian as the ——— Stone.

3. He has also been called the Stone Who ——— Away.

4. Ian was performing at the ——— Arms when he met Mick, Keith, and Brian.

5. True or false: Ian was included on the Stones' early recording of "Come On."

6. Ian plays piano, organ, and ———.

7. He has also served as the Stones' ——— manager.

8. Rather than becoming a full-time member of the Rolling Stones, Ian kept his job at ——— Studios.

9. Ian's musicianship is featured on ———, a song that was withdrawn as the "A" side of "I Wanna Be Your Man" and replaced by "Not Fade Away" for the Stones' first single release in America.

10. True or false: Ian performed with the Stones on their U.S. tour during the summer of 1978.

17. FOURTEEN

A. All the profits from the English sampler album "Fourteen," released in 1963, were donated to what charity?

Match the following groups or individual artists to their respective cuts on the album.

1. The Rolling Stones	a. "Kiss, Kiss"
2. The Bachelors	b. "Baby's in Black"
3. Billy Fury	c. "Little Girl"
4. Tom Jones	d. "Maureen"
5. The Zombies	e. "Just One Look"
6. Unit Four Plus Two	f. "Tomboy"
7. The Applejacks	g. "Nothing's Changed"
8. Lulu and the Luvvers	h. "Surprise, Surprise"
9. Them	i. "This Diamond Ring"
10. The Johnny Howard Band	j. "Women from Liberia"

18. MARIANNE UNFAITHFULL

1. As a result of her friendship with Mick Jagger, Marianne Faithfull eventually split with her husband John———.

2. What is the first name of Marianne's and John's son?

3. Marianne replaced which long-time girlfriend of Mick's?

4. Give the name of the art gallery owned by Marianne's ex-husband.

5. Which member of the Beatles met his future wife at this art gallery?

6. What is the title of the Jagger/Richard song Marianne recorded as her first hit single?

7. What is the flip side of this first single?

8. In what year was the record released? Who served as Marianne's producer?

9. Marianne appeared with the Stones on what special filmed for British television?

10. Marianne made headlines in the British press as the "girl in the——— rug."

19. THE ROLLING STONES' FIRST TOUR

The Stones toured England from September to November 3, 1963. They appeared on the bill (not yet as headliners) with the following acts. Answer true or false after each one.

1. The Walker Brothers
2. The Everly Brothers
3. Bo Diddley
4. "The Dutchess" and Jerome
5. Herman's Hermits
6. Little Richard
7. The Animals
8. Mickie Most
9. Julie Grant
10. Freddie and the Dreamers

20. THE STONES AND THE BEATLES

1. Name the American concert promoter who was responsible for initially bringing over the Beatles and the Rolling Stones to the United States.

2. Identify the accountant/manager who once handled the Beatles and, later, the Stones.

3. Which member of the Beatles saw the Stones early in their career at the Crawdaddy?

4. Name the two members of the Beatles who sang backing vocals on the Stones' record "We Love You."

5. Mick Jagger and Keith Richard sing back-up vocals on the Beatles single "All You Need Is ———."

6. Which member of the Beatles appeared with the Rolling Stones on *Rock 'n' Roll Circus*? Paul McCartney's future wife, Linda Eastman, first photographed the Stones for which American magazine, in the 1960's?

7. Mick Jagger participated in the making of which album by Yoko Ono and the Plastic Ono Band?

8. Brian Jones plays soprano sax on the Beatles single "Baby You're a ——— Man."

9. Both the Beatles and the Rolling Stones worked with producer Phil ——— and Glyn ———.

10. Identify the member of the Rolling Stones and his girlfriend who joined the Beatles for a visit with the Maharishi in 1967.

21. ENGLISH CHANNEL

Fill in the blanks, completing the titles of these English radio and television shows on which the Rolling Stones appeared.

Radio:

1. ——— Club
2. Top ———

   Top ———

Television:

3. Top of the ———
4. Ready, ———, Go!
5. Thank Your ——— Stars
6. Juke Box ———
7. ——— Night at the London Palladium
8. ——— Andrews Show

Television Specials:

9. The Stones in the ———
10. Old ——— Whistle Test

22. MUDDY STONES

1. Name the two superstars of soul (both now deceased) who recorded "Little Red Rooster" in addition to Muddy Waters and the Rolling Stones.

The following songs were all recorded by Muddy Waters as well as by the Rolling Stones. Answer true or false after each title.

2. "Rollin' Stone"

3. "Mannish Boy"

4. "Whiskey Blues"

5. "Train Fare Blues"

6. "I Can't Be Satisfied"

7. "Hoochie Coochie Man"

8. "Let's Spend the Night Together"

9. "I Just Want to Make Love to You"

10. "Big Leg Woman"

23. STONES STARDUST: THE NAME GAME

1. The Rolling Stones once planned to call their record label ——— Earth.

2. Insiders believe that soul singer Claudia ——— inspired the Stones' song "Brown Sugar."

3. The original title of the "Black and Blue" album was "——— Stuff."

4. What was the working title of the song "Sympathy for the Devil"?

5. The first Stones bootleg album, "Liver Than You'll Ever Be," was cut on ——— Records.

6. Name the London Records promotion man thought to have inspired the Stones song "The Under Assistant West Coast Promotion Man."

7. What was the "Let It Bleed" album originally to have been called?

8. The Stones album "Their Satanic Majesties Request" was initially titled "Her Satanic Majesty Requests and ———."

9. The satanic album had first been planned under the title "——— Christmas."

10. Bill Wyman once planned a Stones album of tapes to be called "The ——— Box."

24. STONES: TOP BILLING IS THRILLING

Pebbles no more: The Rolling Stones topped the bill for the first time on this British tour.

1. Give the opening date of their first tour as headliners.

2. First appearance on this tour was at the ——— Cinema, Harrow.

3. Name the American all-girl group that appeared on the bill with the Stones.

4. Identify the record producer that the leader of this female group was married to at one time.

5. Marty ——— was also on the bill with the Stones.

The Rolling Stones first headline tour included the following itinerary of the English countryside. Answer true or false after the name of each area.

6. Kew

7. Tooting

8. Maidstone

9. Chelsea

10. Woolwich

25. SOME OF THE GIRLS

Fill in the blanks, supplying the last names of some of the big girls featured on the former inside sleeve of the Stones' "Some Girls" album.

1. Joey ———
2. Elizabeth ———
3. Gina ———
4. Joan ———
5. Judy ———
6. Jayne ———
7. Brigitte ———
8. Marilyn ———
9. Liza ———
10. Farrah Fawcett ———

26. BOBBY JAGGER?

The Bobby Beat: The Rolling Stones' first American tour opened in San Bernardino, California, in June 1964. Several singers whose first name is Bobby appeared on the same bill with the Stones, including the artists all listed below by their last names as well. Answer true or false after each one in this Bobby Bonanza.

1. Bobby Hatfield
2. Bobby Rydell
3. Bobby Vee
4. Bobby Vinton
5. Bobby Sherman
6. Bobby Baer
7. Bobby Goldsboro
8. Bobby Hebb
9. Bobby Comstock
10. Bobby Darin

27. MALICE ON HOLLYWOOD PALACE

1. Give the month and year of the Rolling Stones' appearance on *Hollywood Palace.*

2. Upon introducing the Stones, host Dean Martin held his ———.

3. Dean declared the Stones' hair was not long: "It's just smaller ——— and higher ———."

4. What two songs did the Stones perform on *Hollywood Palace*?

5. According to Dean Martin, the Stones were going back to England to have a hair-pulling contest with what group?

6. Dean introduced a trampoline artist as the ——— of the Rolling Stones, adding, "He's been trying to ——— himself ever since."

7. Name Dean Martin's former comedy partner.

8. Along with Frank Sinatra, Sammy Davis, Jr., and Peter Lawford, Dean and his pals became known in the press as the ——— Pack.

9. Dean's son and namesake was once a member of a rock group called Dino, ———, and Billy.

10. This son, now an actor, bills himself as Dean ——— Martin. Identify his ex-wife, an English actress, and the former Olympic figure-skating champion he dates.

28. BRIAN'S DEATH: July 3, 1969

1. Give the date Brian officially quit the Rolling Stones.

2. Brian lived at historic ——— Farm in Sussex at the time of his death.

3. This farm was once the home of author A. A. Milne, who wrote the classic *Winnie the* ———.

4. Where was Brian's body discovered?

5. As a result of her efforts to revive Brian, his nurse was called "The Kiss of ——— Girl" by some English newspapers.

6. The coroner's report on Brian declared, "Death by ———."

7. How old was Brian at the time of his death?

8. Brian's epitaph: "Please Don't Judge Me Too ——."

9. What Rolling Stones album was packaged in memory of Brian?

10. Name the song Pete Townshend of the Who wrote about Brian after learning of his death.

29. STONE STUMPERS

1. An English music paper called the Stones a "———-like quintet" early in the group's career.

2. Mick Jagger sang a duet with Peter Tosh in concert at New York's Palladium during the summer of 1978. What is the name of the song?

3. This duet with Mick was later recorded for inclusion in a Peter Tosh album called "——— Doctor."

4. Identify the two executive producers of the Peter Tosh album.

5. Peter Tosh was formerly a member of what reggae band headed by Bob Marley?

6. Give the title of the song Phil Spector wrote with the Stones.

7. The Rolling Stones recorded "Poison Ivy," a song made famous originally by what group?

8. Who is "Uncle Gene" on the Stones' recording "Now I've Got a Witness (Like Uncle Phil and Uncle Gene)"?

9. Chrissie Shrimpton once left Mick Jagger for English singer P. J. ———.

10. Name the Buddy Holly hit released by the Stones in 1964.

30. BACK IN THE U.S.A.: STONES' AMERICAN TOURS

Fill in the blanks, giving the years of the Stones' American tours, listed below in chronological order. Some years include more than one U.S. tour.

1. First American tour: June ———
2. Second American tour: October–November ———
3. Third American tour: April–May ———
4. Fourth American tour: October, November–December ———
5. Fifth American tour: June–July, ———
6. Sixth American tour: November ———
7. Seventh American tour: June–July ———
8. Hawaii: January ———
9. Tour of the Americas: June–July–August ———
10. Surprise tour: June–July, ———

31. (OTIS) REDDING HEADING

The following songs were all recorded by Otis Redding as well as by the Rolling Stones. Answer true or false after each title.

1. "Pain in My Heart"
2. "Respect"
3. "(I Can't Get No) Satisfaction"
4. "Dock of the Bay"
5. "I've Been Loving You Too Long"
6. "My Girl"
7. "Love Man"
8. "That's How Strong My Love Is"
9. "You Made a Man Out of Me"
10. "Try a Little Tenderness"

32. THE BRIAN JONES MEMORIAL CONCERT

1. Give the date of the memorial concert in Brian's honor.

2. This free concert was held at London's ——— Park.

3. The crowd was estimated in round numbers at approximately ———,000 fans.

4. Give the last name of the poet whose work Mick Jagger read to the audience in memory of Brian.

5. Specifically, Mick read stanzas 39 and 52 from the poem ———.

6. To further honor Brian, Mick released hundreds of white ———.

Fill in the blanks, completing the names of the following acts that also appeared on the program.

7. King ———.

8. Third ——— Band.

9. ——— Ornaments.

10. Alexis Korner's group, ——— Church.

33. (CHUCK) BERRY PICKING WITH THE STONES

The Rolling Stones recorded the following songs, all written by Chuck Berry. Did Berry actually write every one of these songs? Answer true or false after each title.

1. "Around and Around"
2. "You Can't Catch Me"
3. "Route 66"
4. "Little Queenie"
5. "Fortune Teller"
6. "Talkin' 'Bout You"
7. "Play with Fire"
8. "Come On"
9. "Bye Bye Johnny"
10. "It's All Over Now"

34. MICK: TAYLOR MADE

1. Give the date of the press conference held to officially announce Mick Taylor joining the Rolling Stones.

2. Which member of the Stones did he replace?

3. What is the date of Mick's birth?

4. Identify his sun sign.

5. Before devoting full time to the guitar, Mick worked briefly as an artist ——.

6. Mick was once photographed performing at a concert wearing an ——— wig.

7. In what year did Mick appear on an American tour with the Stones for the first time?

8. Mick was a member of the Rolling Stones for approximately ——— and a half years.

9. He left the Stones in December of what year?

10. Who replaced Mick Taylor?

35. THE STONES LOVE YOU

1. In what year was the single "We Love You" released?

2. "——— Summer" is the title of the single the Rolling Stones had originally intended to release instead of "We Love You."

3. What is the B side of "We Love You"?

4. Peter ——— directed the promotional English telefilm for "We Love You."

5. The telefilm was an adaptation of *The Trials of Oscar* ———.

6. Identify the character Mick Jagger portrayed.

7. Keith was cast as the Marquess of ———.

8. Who is the female pop singer featured in this project?

9. Indicate the role she plays.

10. The director of the telefilm also directed the Rolling Stones in two movies. Give their titles.

36. THE ROLLING STONES ROCK 'N' ROLL CIRCUS

1. *Rock 'n' Roll Circus* was originally made for what medium?

2. Give the month and year *Rock 'n' Roll Circus* was filmed.

3. Name the real circus featured.

4. What circus role did Mick Jagger play?

5. Yoko Ono appeared dressed as a ———.

6. She sang to the accompaniment of what famed violinist?

7. *Rock 'n' Roll Circus* was originally intended as the Rolling Stones' answer to which Beatles film?

8. The circus project was directed by Michael Lindsay-Hogg. Name the Beatles film he also directed.

9. Michael Lindsay-Hogg is the son of what well-known actress?

10. Identify the song Marianne Faithful sang in *Rock 'n' Roll Circus* which was written by Carole King and Gerry Goffin.

37. STONES' SUPERSOUL

Match the following songs to the individual artists and groups who originally recorded them before the Stones.

1. "Hitch Hike"	a. Wilson Pickett
2. "Ain't Too Proud to Beg"	b. Irma Thomas
3. "Under the Boardwalk"	c. Barrett Strong
4. "I'm a King Bee"	d. Marvin Gaye
5. "Let It Rock"	e. Solomon Burke
6. "Money"	f. The Drifters
7. "Walking the Dog"	g. Chuck Berry
8. "Time Is on My Side"	h. The Temptations
9. "Everybody Needs Somebody to Love"	i. Rufus Thomas
10. "If You Need Me"	j. Slim Harpo

38. BLACK AND BLUES

Fill in the blanks, completing the following song titles written and/or recorded by the Rolling Stones, including a revised title of an X-rated song and a bootleg cut; the title of a Stones album; and a tune performed by the supergroup in Rock 'n' Roll Circus, *which included a member of the Stones.*

1. "I ——— the Blues"
2. "——— the Blues"
3. "——— Blues"
4. "Sweet Black ———"
5. "——— It Black"
6. "Blue Turns to ———"
7. "——— and Blue"
8. "Bluesberry ———" (bootleg cut)
9. "——— Blues" (tune performed by the supergroup in *Rock 'n' Roll Circus*)
10. "——— Blues" (revised title of an X-rated Stones song)

39. ED SULLIVAN: THE STONES MEET OLD STONE-FACE

1. The Rolling Stones were turned down for an appearance on *The Ed Sullivan Show* during their first American tour and were seen on what TV show instead?

2. Give the date of the Stones' first performance on the Sullivan show.

3. After the Stones caused fans to riot in the studio, Ed Sullivan vowed, "I promise you they'll ——— be back on our show."

4. What was the date of the Stones' second appearance on the Sullivan show?

5. As a result of the first riots, Ed Sullivan declared, "We'll ban ——— from the theater if we have to." How did Mick Jagger alter the title of "Let's Spend the Night Together" for Sullivan's audience?

6. Name the English group Ed Sullivan called "nice fellows" and "gentlemen" in contrast to the Stones.

7. The Stones were recommended by Ed Sullivan's ——— in England.

8. When did Sullivan see the Stones for the first time?

9. He was "———" at the sight of them.

10. Angered by the riots the Stones caused, Ed Sullivan declared he would not have his show destroyed in a matter of weeks. For it took him "——— years to build this show."

40. BIANCA: BROWN SUGAR

1. Give Bianca's full maiden name.

2. What is the full name Bianca gave on the marriage certificate when she wed Mick?

3. Identify the city in which Bianca originally met Mick at a party after a Stones concert.

4. She was said to have once been engaged to what record-company executive?

5. Before meeting Mick, Bianca was also romantically linked with actor Michael ———.

6. In what country was Bianca born?

7. Name the American designer who frequently serves as Bianca's escort.

8. Trendy Bianca often carried a ——— stick.

9. One of the sons of which incumbent president showed Bianca around the White House during the Stones' American tour in 1975?

10. In 1976, Bianca bowed out of a role in what movie? Some of the scenes in the film were too ———, Bianca claimed.

41. STONE ALBUMS: SAME DIFFERENCE?

The following Rolling Stone albums contain all the same tracks on both the English and American versions. Answer true or false after the title of each album.

1. "Beggars Banquet"
2. "Out of Our Heads"
3. "Let It Bleed"
4. "It's Only Rock 'n' Roll"
5. "Between the Buttons"
6. "Black and Blue"
7. "Through the Past, Darkly"
8. "Aftermath"
9. "Get Yer Ya-Ya's Out!"
10. "Exile on Main Street"

42. MICK'S MARRIAGE (Here Comes Bianca the Bride)

1. Give Mick's and Bianca's wedding date.

2. Identify the resort town where they were married.

3. Name the two witnesses to the wedding ceremony at the local town hall.

4. Mick housed his wedding guests at the Hotel ———.

5. Indicate the church where the blessing was conferred.

6. The church ceremony was performed by Abbé Lucien ———.

7. Bianca was escorted down the aisle by Lord ———.

8. Music at the ceremony included Bianca's request for the theme from what movie?

9. Mick took instruction in ——— to prepare for his marriage.

10. The wedding reception was held at the Café des ———.

43. KEITH: POP GOES THE SYMPHONY

The Aranbee Pop Symphony Orchestra album on Immediate Records was produced and directed by Keith Richard. Match the songs on the album to their respective writers. Some writers are represented by more than one song.

1. "Rag Doll"	a. Jagger, Richard
2. "I Don't Want to Go On Without You"	b. Lennon, McCartney
3. "Play with Fire"	c. Berns, Wexler
4. "In the Midnight Hour"	d. Crewe, Gaudio
5. "Sittin' on a Fence"	e. Sonny Bono
6. "We Can Work It Out"	f. Pickett, Cropper
7. "Take It or Leave It"	
8. "I Got You Babe"	
9. "There's a Placc"	
10. "Mother's Little Helper"	

44. MR. & MRS. MICK: WEDDING-GUEST LIST

Heading for a wedding: The following attended Mick's and Bianca's wedding. Answer true or false after each name.

1. Ringo Starr
2. Brian Jones
3. Paul and Linda McCartney
4. Dave Clark
5. Ossie Clark
6. Keith Richard
7. Mick's parents
8. Bianca's parents
9. Mick's brother
10. Bianca's sister

45. STONE SUPPER: CRITICS EAT CROW

Fill in the blanks, completing the titles of this varied menu of songs. Many courses of spicy food and drink are included: a Rolling Stones tune and the title of one of the Stones albums; cuts from albums by Leon Russell, Dr. John, and Herbie Mann on which some members of the Rolling Stones perform as session guests; and tracks from a Bill Wyman solo album and a Tucky Buzzard album produced by Bill.

1. "Goat's Head ———"
2. "Pots on Fiyo (Filé ———)"
3. "——— of the Earth"
4. "Pisces ——— Lady"
5. "——— Butter Time"
6. "Memphis Spoon ——— & Dover Sole"
7. "Craney ———"
8. "——— and Wimmen"
9. "She's ———"
10. "——— Eyes"

46. SUPERSTARS SING THE STONES

Under the covers: Yes, match these top artists to the titles of their cover records of Stones hits. Two of the songs indicated here have been recorded by more than one of the singers listed.

1. Melanie
2. Peter Frampton
3. Otis Redding
4. Judy Collins
5. Rod Stewart
6. George Burns
7. Leon Russell
8. Joe Cocker
9. Joan Baez
10. Johnny Winter

a. "(I Can't Get No) Satisfaction"
b. "Street Fighting Man"
c. "Honky Tonk Women"
d. "Jumpin' Jack Flash"
e. "No Expectations"
f. "Ruby Tuesday"
g. "Salt of the Earth"

47. JADE ON PARADE

1. Does Jade Jagger have a middle name?

2. If their firstborn had been a boy, Bianca was keen on the name ——— James.

3. What is the date of Jade's birth?

4. Indicate her sun sign.

5. Jade was born at the ——— Nursing Home.

6. In what city is this nursing home located?

7. To celebrate Jade's birth, Mick threw a ——— party.

8. Mick won't allow Jade to be ———.

9. Did Mick and Bianca have any other children together?

10. Mick is quoted as saying he is a "———" dad.

48. GIRLS! GIRLS! GIRLS! (& Some Motherly Types, Too)

Fill in the blanks, completing the titles of these Stones recordings about big girls.

1. "Down ——— Girl"

2. "——— Girl"
   "——— Girl"
   "——— Girl"

3. "——— Woman"

4. "Mother's Little ———"

5. "——— Mama"

6. "Honky ——— Women"

7. "———Street Girl"

8. "———, Little Sister"

9. "——— Girls"

10. "Have You Seen Your Mother, Baby, Standing in the ———?"

49. BRIDGE OVER MUDDY WATERS

1. What is Muddy Waters' real name?

2. Give his date of birth.

3. Muddy's song "——— Stone" was said to have influenced Brian Jones and the rest of the group in the final choice of the group's name.

4. The Stones first met Muddy in the United States when they recorded at ——— Studios.

5. What was the year of this historic meeting?

6. The famed recording complex was located in what city?

7. Identify the two other top blues musicians present at the Stones recording session.

8. During their American tour, Mick Jagger and three other members of the Stones jammed with Muddy. In what month and year did this event take place?

9. Name the club and the city where the Stones made music with Muddy.

10. Which member of the Stones was not present for the jam?

50. SOME GIRLS: SOME STONE FACTS

1. What color stripe near the top of the "Some Girls" sleeve is the rarest?

2. ——— is the second rarest color to find under the heading.

3. Give the four price categories of the wigs advertised on the album sleeve.

4. Lucille ——— registered a strong protest against the use of her photo on the "Some Girls" album sleeve, and the cover was subsequently changed so as not to offend any of the "girls."

5. Actress ——— Welch also complained about the original cover.

6. The ads on the "Some Girls" sleeve are similar to those featured by ——— of Hollywood.

7. Name the one song on the "Some Girls" album not written by Mick Jagger and Keith Richard.

8. The back cover of the album highlights ads for ———.

9. Much of the album was cut at E.M.I. Studios in what city?

10. Name the three nonmembers of the Stones featured on the "Miss You" track and the instruments they play.

51. STONES MACHO MEN & BOYS

Fill in the blanks, completing the titles of these songs showing the Stones macho and some not so.

1. "Jumpin' ——— Flash"
2. "I'd ——— Rather Be with the Boys"
3. "The —— Assistant West Coast Promotion Man"
4. "——— Boy"
5. "Dancing With Mr. ———"
6. "Street ——— Man"
7. "Roll Over ———"
8. "Bye Bye ———"
9. "Memo from ———"
10. "I ——— Be Your Man"

52. BILL MEETS THE BUZZARD (And a Swarm of Other Talent)

1. Among the Tucky Buzzard albums produced by Bill Wyman are "Warm ——" and "——— on the Night."

2. The earlier version of Tucky Buzzard was a group called the ———, also produced by Bill.

3. Bill co-produced a single featuring John Lee's Groundhogs with ——— Johns, who co-produced the Beatles' "Let It Be" album.

Bill Wyman also produced singles by the following groups. Answer true or false after each name.

4. Chelsea Morning

5. The Warren Davis Monday Band

6. Hamilton and the Movement

7. The Big Ben

8. Moon's Train

9. The Union Jack

10. The Preachers

53. TH ROLLING STONES COLORING BOOK

Fill in the blanks, completing the titles of these colorful songs. In addition to Rolling Stones tunes (and the title of a Stones album) are tracks from albums by Dr. John and Herbie Mann, which each include a member of the Rolling Stones as a session guest; tracks from albums by Tucky Buzzard and the End, produced by Bill Wyman; and a selection from one of Bill's solo albums.

1. "——— Sugar"
2. "You Got the ———"
3. "——— Lightnin' "
4. "A ——— Shade of Pale"
5. "Shades of ———"
6. "——— John the Conqueror"
7. "Mellow ———"
8. "——— Train"
9. "Big Hits (High Tide and ——— Grass)"
10. "——— Medallions"

54. MARGARET TRUDEAU: MICK, CLICK, & FLICK

1. Margaret photographed the Rolling Stones during their performance at Canada's El ——.

2. In what province is this club located?

3. It was widely reported that Margaret was out with Mick Jagger and the rest of the Rolling Stones on her —— wedding anniversary.

4. Her estranged husband, Pierre Trudeau, is —— minister of Canada.

5. How many years older than Margaret is Pierre?
6. Margaret and Pierre are the parents of —— children.
7. Give the first names of their kids.

8. Identify the title of Margaret's first movie.

9. Who is her leading man in this film?

10. The Trudeau's official government residence is 24 —— Drive in Ottawa, the Canadian equivalent of the U.S. White House.

55. ROCK 'N' ROLL LADIES

Fill in the blanks, completing the titles of these songs performed (and some written) by the Stones celebrating womanhood. Bootleg releases count here.

1. "——— Q."
2. "Lady ———"
3. "Miss ——— Jones"
4. "Downtown ———"
5. "Little ———"
6. "Sweet ———"
7. "——— Tuesday"
8. "Jiving Sister ———"
9. "Beautiful ———"
10. "Fanny ———"

56. IMMEDIATE SUCCESS, STONES STYLE

The following artists are correctly matched with the Jagger/Richard tunes they recorded for Andrew Oldham's label, Immediate Records. Answer true or false after each name.

1. The Herd—"So Much In Love"
2. Nicky Scott—"Back-Street Girl"
3. George Bean—"Will You Be My Lover Tonight?"
4. The Mighty Avengers—"Blue Turns to Grey"
5. Charles Dickens—"So Much in Love"
6. The Greenbeats—"You Must Be the One"
7. Jimmy Tarbuck—"Wasting Time"
8. Thee—"Each and Every Day"
9. Twice as Much—"Sittin' on a Fence"
10. Bobby Jameson—"All I Want Is My Baby"

STONES PHOTO QUIZ

1. The group briefly called themselves the ________ Rolling Stones.

2. Beatlestones: Early in their career, the Rolling Stones had a hit record with what song written by the Beatles?

(Answers to the STONES PHOTO QUIZ appear on page 154)

3. June 2, 1964: Helen Rosenbaum, author of this quiz book, interviews the Rolling Stones at their first American press conference held in New York's __________ Hotel.

   P.S.—Mick no longer sits at her feet.

   P.P.S.—The hotel has since been torn down.

4. The Rolling Stones collaborated on songs under the names Naker, __________. Where does The Under Assistant West Coast promotion man wait for a bus?

5. Name the other Stones album with the word "Live" in the title.

6. Unbuttoned: Which member of the Stones drew the cartoons featured on the back of the "Between The Buttons" album sleeve?

7. Brian Jones died on July 3, 1969. Name the sexy lead singer who died on that date exactly two years later. Identify this rock star's group.

8. Mick Taylor played guitar with what group before joining the Stones?

9. Lonesome cowboy: Who is the outlaw Mick Jagger portrays in the title role of this film?

10. Weekend Warrior: What is the name of Mick's Elizabethan Manor, which once served as Oliver Cromwell's military headquarters?

11. Name the actress pictured with Mick in *Performance*. Which Rolling Stone is she married to in real life? What movie did she appear in with Ringo Starr?

12. Pucker up: Critics have variously described this chap's lips as __________ Lips and __________ Lips.

13. Soul Brothers: Mick and Keith share record production credits as the __________ Twins.

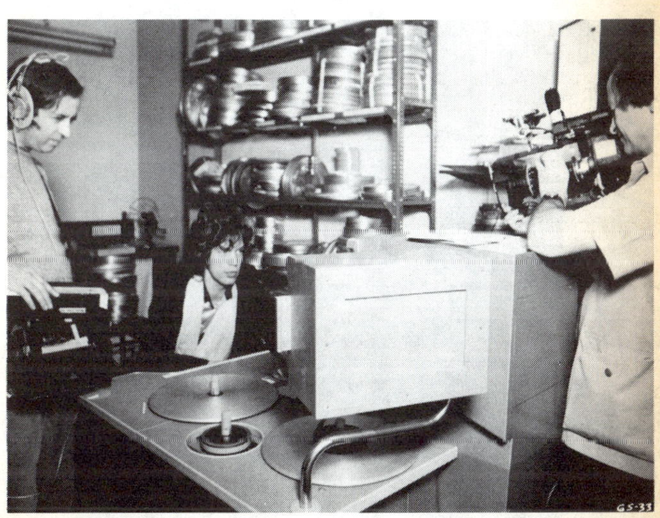

14. Reel Brothers: Give the full names of the brothers who directed *Gimme Shelter*, shown here with Mick. Name the woman who co-directed the film.

15. Jumpsuit Jack Flash: Which university did Mick attend for two years?

16. What's the exact time of the special disco version of "Miss You"?

57. CHRIS JAGGER: SOUL BROTHER #1

1. Chris is ——— years younger than Mick.
2. Identify the English suburb where Chris and Mick grew up.
3. Does Chris have any other brothers or sisters?
4. In what year was the album "Chris Jagger" released?
5. Who co-produced the album with Chris?
6. In what capacity was Mick heard on his brother's album?
7. Drummer Roger ——— played on the album cut "Handful of Dust."
8. Name this drummer's current group.
9. Swedish actress Britt ——— was briefly linked with this drummer.
10. The actress was formerly married to English actor Peter ——— and later became the longtime girl friend of rock star ——— Stewart.

58. STONE SKELETONS: ANATOMY LESSON

Fill in the blanks, completing the titles of these Stones songs and album titles with heart and soul, mind and body.

1. "Pain in My ———"
2. "——— File"
3. "Under My ———"
4. "Sticky ———"
5. "——— of Stone"
6. "Shake Your ———"
7. "——— of Fate"
8. "Far-Away ———"
9. "Some Things Just Stick in Your ———"
10. "Out of Our ———"

59. MICK TAYLOR REPLACEMENT-RUMOR MATCH-UP

Match the first names to the last names of the guitarists, all rumored at one time or another to be the replacement for Mick Taylor before the Stones found reason to knock on (Ron) Wood.

1. Harvey	a. Johnson
2. Leslie	b. Frampton
3. Chris	c. Marriott
4. Shuggie	d. Mandel
5. Wayne	e. Beck
6. Steve	f. Spedding
7. Jimmy	g. Perkins
8. Peter	h. West
9. Wilco	i. Page
10. Jeff	j. Otis

60. STONE LOVE

Fill in the blanks, completing the loving thoughts in these songs recorded and mostly written by the Stones.

1. "Will You Be My Lover ———?"
2. "That's How ——— My Love Is"
3. "Loving ———"
4. "I Just Want to ——— Love to You"
5. "Love in ———"
6. "I've Been Loving You Too ———"
7. "——— Your Love"
8. "We Love ———"
9. "Everybody Needs ——— to Love"
10. "So ——— in Love"

61. CHRIS: A TOUGH ACT FOR MICK TO FARLOWE?

1. Mick Jagger produced the album "The ——— of Chris Farlowe."

2. Name Mick's two co-producers for the album "Farlowe in the Midnight Hour."

3. Chris Farlowe recorded for ——— Records.

4. Who was Andrew Oldham's partner in this record company?

Mick Jagger produced singles recorded by Chris Farlowe of the following Jagger/Richard tunes. Answer true or false after each song title.

5. "Ride On, Baby"

6. "She's a Rainbow"

7. "Paint It Black"

8. "Yesterday's Papers"

9. "Play with Fire"

10. "Out of Time"

62: RON: OUT OF THE WOODWORK

1. What is Ron Wood's nickname?

2. Give Ron's date of birth.

3. Give his sun sign.

4. Ron was an original member of the Jeff ——— Group.

5. He established himself with what other group before joining the Rolling Stones?

6. Name Ron's first album as a solo artist.

7. Identify the three members of the Rolling Stones who backed Ron on various tracks of his first album.

8. In what year was this album released?

9. Give the title of Ron's second solo album.

10. In what year did Ron appear on an American tour with the Stones for the first time?

63. STONES ALBUM CALENDAR

Match the following English and American album releases by the Rolling Stones to the year of their release.

1. "Metamorphosis"	a. 1964
2. "Flowers"	b. 1965
3. "Stone Age"	c. 1966
4. "December's Children"	d. 1967
5. "Some Girls"	e. 1968
6. "Beggars Banquet"	f. 1969
7. "12×5"	g. 1971
8. "Let It Bleed"	h. 1972
9. "Hot Rocks: 1964–1971"	i. 1975
10. "Big Hits (High Tide and Green Grass)"	j. 1978

64. STONES FLIP THEIR WIGS

The following wig stlyes are "advertised" on the sleeve of the Rolling Stones' "Some Girls" album. Answer true or false after the name of each wig.

1. London Look
2. Wiz-Wig
3. Freedom Wig
4. Lovin' Wig
5. Afro
6. Dutch Boy
7. Beau Catcher
8. Cleopatra
9. Gypsy
10. Georgie Girl

65. BILLY PRESTON ISN'T COUNTRY & WESTERN

1. Give the years of Billy Preston's two American tours with the Rolling Stones.
2. What are the titles of Billy's two albums on Apple?
3. Name the film in which Billy appeared with the Bee Gees and Peter Frampton.
4. Identify the song Billy once recorded with the Beatles that he also sings in this movie.
5. Billy performed at the Concert for ———Desh.
6. Name the record company Billy joined after his departure from Apple.
7. Early in his career Billy cut an album with Ray Charles entitled "The Most Exciting ——— Ever."
8. On the Beatles' "Let It Be" sessions, Billy played ——— piano.
9. Which member of the Beatles served as Billy's producer at Apple?
10. "——— from Nothing" was a big hit single for Billy.

66. CIRCUS DROPOUTS

The Rolling Stones had originally wanted to use the following acts in Rock 'n' Roll Circus. *Answer true or false after each name.*

1. Jimi Hendrix
2. Johnny Cash
3. Dr. John
4. The Electric Prunes
5. The Electric Flag
6. Traffic
7. The Electric Light Orchestra
8. The Isley Brothers
9. Sonny & Cher
10. Spooky Tooth

67. JERRY: HALL OF FAME

1. Name the British rock singer Jerry Hall was engaged to before meeting Mick Jagger. Give the title of her former fiancé's cover record of a Stones' hit.

2. What is Jerry's middle name?

3. Give the first and middle names of Jerry's twin sister.

4. Identify the state in which Jerry was born and raised.

5. In what city did Jerry first gain success as a model?

6. How many sisters does Jerry have in addition to her twin?

7. Jerry's nickname was "——— Hall."

8. Identify the film in which Jerry had a walk-on part that was later cut.

9. What is the most frequent misspelling of Jerry's name in the press?

10. Mick reportedly gifted Jerry with a ——— bracelet for her twenty-second birthday.

68. EDWARD & THE STONES

1. Name the three members of the Rolling Stones on the "Jamming with Edward" album.

2. In what year was the album released?

3. Who wrote the letter of apology accompanying the album upon its release?

4. Nicky Hopkins jammed with the three Stones on the album. What is Nicky's pet name?

5. Musician Ry ——— is also featured on the album.

6. Identify the Rolling Stones film in which Ry plays on the soundtrack.

Fill in the blanks, completing the titles of these cuts co-written by Charlie Watts from "Jamming With Edward."

7. "The ——— Stomp."

8. "——— Thrump Up."

9. "Blow with ———."

10. "——— Fling."

69. HEY, MICK AND KEITH, WRITE ME A SONG

Several of the following Jagger/Richard compositions were originally written for and/or recorded by others. Match the individual artist or group to their early recording of a Stones song.

1. The Who	a. "Let It Bleed"
2. Gene Pitney	b. "Surprise, Surprise"
3. The Searchers	c. "Congratulations"
4. Lulu and the Luvvers	d. "Shang a Doo Lang"
5. The Flying Burrito Brothers	e. "The Last Time"
6. Cliff Richard and the Shadows	f. "Some Things Just Stick in Your Mind"
7. West Five	g. "Take It or Leave It"
8. Johnny Winter	h. "Wild Horses"
9. Vashti	i. "That Girl Belongs to Yesterday"
10. Adrienne Poster	j. "Blue Turns to Grey"

70. STONES SUMMER SECRETS OF '78 (The American Tour)

1. Tickets for a Stones concert in Florida were sold under the guise of The Great Southeast Stoned-Out —— Champions.

2. While the Stones were appearing at the Capitol Theater in Passaic, New Jersey, the marquee proclaimed, "Closed for ——."

3. Mick Jagger claimed the Stones never play —— but proved otherwise in Passaic.

4. The Stones were billed as what insect group to some ticket buyers in Atlanta and Washington?

5. Ian ——, formerly of Faces, joined the Stones on tour at the last minute.

6. Face in the Crowd: What is Ian's nickname?

7. Identify the Philadelphia Stadium named after a former United States President where the Stones played to a capacity audience of more than 90,000 fans.

8. The Stones turned up in Atlanta to do a concert at the —— Theater.

9. In Washington, D.C., the Stones played the —— Theater.

10. The group also did a show at the —— in Manhattan.

71. CARLY SIMON: LOVE IN VAIN

1. Mick Jagger sings vocal ——— on Carly's recording of "You're So Vain."

2. What is the B side of this single?

3. While "You're So Vain" was thought to be about Mick, identify the actor some claimed really inspired this song.

4. The song was recorded for ——— Records.

5. In what year was the single released?

6. Who produced "You're So Vain"?

7. Identify the two Carly Simon albums on which "You're So Vain" appears.

8. Carly is married to singer James ———.

9. What are the first names of their two children?

10. Carly's older sister, ——— Simon, is a famed opera singer.

72. STONES' BOOTLEG BONANZA

The following are titles of Stones bootleg albums. Answer true or false after each one.

1. "Exiles on Seven Sisters Road"
2. "Get Your Leeds Lungs Out"
3. "Watts Cooking"
4. "We Never Really Got It On till Detroit"
5. "Jaggered Edge"
6. "No Cryin' for Brian"
7. "Sympathy for Angie"
8. "Nicaraguan Earthquake Benefit Concert"
9. "Mickey Mouth"
10. "The Stars in the Sky—They Never Lie"

73. HOWLIN' WITH THE STONES

1. "The London Howlin' Wolf Sessions" album was released in what year?

2. What is Howlin' Wolf's real name?

3. Name the sometime Stone who plays piano on several of the album cuts.

4. Identify the two full-time members of the Stones also heard instrumentally on the album.

5. One of the Stones is credited with playing the —— bell plus brass and shakers on the album tracks.

6. Stevie ———, formerly of the Spencer Davis Group and Traffic, is a featured musician on the album.

7. What is the name of the album's lead guitarist? Together with Stevie, this guitarist was a member of ——— Faith.

8. In addition to singing, Howlin' Wolf plays acoustic guitar and ——— on his London Sessions album.

9. Heavy Howlin': Which member of the Beatles was highlighted on the cut "I Ain't Superstitious"?

10. Give the date of Howlin' Wolf's death.

74. STICKS AND STONES

1. Critics of the Stones refer to their sound as ——— music.
2. In 1972, Mick Jagger was quoted as saying he would quit show business at what age?
3. Early in their career, the Stones appeared on the same bill as Goldie and the Gingerbreads. What is the full name of the real Goldie, now a solo performer? What group did she sing lead with after the Gingerbreads?
4. The Rolling Stones have been called the ——— rock and roll band in the world.
5. Lulu along with the Luvvers recorded the Stones' "Surprise, Surprise." What is the full name of the real Lulu? Identify the rock star she was formerly married to and the name of her ex-husband's group.
6. Stevie ——— was featured on the Stones' tour of the United States in 1972. Give Stevie's first and last name.
7. Name the singer/actor who recorded the novelty tune "Blame It on the Stones." He appears on an album with the original score from which Mick Jagger movie?
8. Long-time publicist for the Stones has been Les ———.
9. The percussionist on the Stones' American tour in 1975 was ——— Brown.
10. An import of the Stones' single "Miss You" backed with "Far-Away Eyes" has been pressed on shocking ——— vinyl. Mick Jagger claims the Stones are "the best ——— band of all."

75. ME & THE STONES

Fill in the blanks, completing the titles of these "me" songs performed and mostly written by the Stones.

1. "——— Bother Me"
2. "If You Can't ——— Me"
3. "Just My ——— (Running Away with Me)"
4. "——— with Me"
5. "Don't ——— to Me"
6. "You Can't ——— Me"
7. "——— to Me"
8. "If You ——— Me"
9. "——— Me"
10. "If You ——— Me"

76. MAGICAL MYSTERY TOUR TALENT

(Rolling Stone Summer in the States, 1978)

1. Linda Ronstadt recorded a cover version of the Stones hit she later performed on stage with the group in Tucson. Give the title of the song.

The following acts appeared on the bill with the Stones during at least one American tour date in 1978. Answer true or false after each name.

2. Marsha Hunt
3. Doug Kershaw
4. Etta James
5. Bruce Springsteen
6. Peter Tosh
7. Dolly Parton
8. Boston
9. Foreigner
10. Billy Joel

77. SUPERGROUP SCOOP: SINGING THE STONES

1. Name the Rolling Stones song recorded by Eric Burdon and War.

2. Eric Burdon was formerly the lead singer with what English group in the early 1960s?

3. The ——— Boys recorded "Tell Me."

4. Identify the two Rolling Stones songs recorded by Rotary Connection.

5. Name the former member of Rotary Connection who went on to record several hits as a solo performer.

6. Give the title of the Stones song recorded by Blood, Sweat, and Tears.

7. Who replaced Al Cooper as vocalist with Blood, Sweat, and Tears?

8. "Dead Flowers" was recorded by New Riders of the ——— Sage.

9. The Who recorded "The Last Time" backed by what other Stones song on the flip side of the single?

10. Give the title of the Stones tune covered by Devo.

78. THE ROLLING STONES ROCK 'N' ROLL CIRCUS ACT

The following single artists and groups appeared with the Stones on Rock 'n' Roll Circus, *originally filmed as a special intended for British television. Did these acts all really appear on the show? Answer true or false after each name.*

1. Ringo Starr
2. Alice Cooper
3. The Who
4. Kiss
5. John Lennon
6. Jethro Tull
7. Paul McCartney
8. Mitch Mitchell
9. George Harrison
10. Eric Clapton

79. MARSHA: BIG-GAME HUNT

1. What is the first name of Marsha Hunt's daughter?

2. Give the child's date of birth.

3. Before she brought suit, how much was Mick Jagger paying Marsha in weekly child support?

4. Marsha went to court asking that the child-support payments be raised to over $———,000 per month.

5. Marsha's daughter was born in St. ——— Hospital, Paddington, England.

6. What is the child's sun sign?

7. Marsha formerly appeared in the English-stage production of what American rock musical?

8. She was also cast in *Catch My Soul*, a rock musical based on what Shakespearean drama?

9. Give the nickname Marsha used in signing her love letters to Mick.

10. Pending the outcome of the child-support suit, a Court prohibited Mick from withdrawing his concert earnings from what state on the Stones' American tour in 1978?

80. ROLLING STONES RECORDS

1. Identify the first Stones album released on Rolling Stones Records.

2. What was the year of the album's release?

3. Name the A side of the Stones' first single on Rolling Stones Records.

4. Indicate the extra song included on the British single only.

5. ——— Chess (whose father co-founded Chess Records) was hired to head Rolling Stones Records. Earl ——— later became president of Rolling Stones Records.

6. Give the name of the Stones' rock documentary co-produced by Marshall.

7. Rolling Stones Records is distributed by ——— Recording Corporation.

8. The logo for Rolling Stones Records features a lapping ———.

9. Who designed this logo?

10. Which member of the Stones cut a solo album for Rolling Stones Records released in 1974?

81. STONES ON TV: TUNE IN, TURN ON

Match the Rolling Stones songs to the TV show they performed them in as recorded on the bootleg album "Summer Re-Runs" issued in 1966. Some shows are represented by more than one song and the Ed Sullivan tracks span several appearances.

1. "Dancing with Mr. D"
2. "Get Off of My Cloud"
3. "Around and Around"
4. You Can't Always Get What You Want"
5. "Angie"
6. "Not Fade Away"
7. "Let's Spend the Night Together"
8. "She Said Yeah"
9. "Silver Train"
10. "As Tears Go By"

a. *Ed Sullivan Show*

b. *David Frost Show*

c. *Hollywood Palace*

d. *Don Kirshner's Rock Concert*

e. *Hullabaloo*

82. REELING AND DEALING ON THE CUTTING-ROOM FLOOR

The Rolling Stones were once linked to the following films that they either turned down or abandoned early on. Answer true or false after each title.

1. *Only Lovers Left Alive*
2. *Back, Behind, and in Front*
3. *The Rolling Stones Meet Dracula*
4. *A Clockwork Orange*
5. *Stone Soul Picnic*
6. *The Maxigasm*

Mick-Nix Flicks

Mick Jagger reportedly turned down roles in the following films. Answer true or false after each title.

7. *The Virgin Soldiers*
8. *Joe Bunch and All That Glitters*
9. *The Mick Jagger Story*
10. *Stranger in a Strange Land*

83. SOME BOYS

The following big boys were pictured on the inside sleeve of the Stones' "Some Girls" album. Answer true or false after each name.

1. Desi Arnez
2. Sonny Bono
3. Joe Namath
4. Red Buttons
5. Mark Heron
6. Lee Majors
7. Joe DiMaggio
8. George Harrison
9. Billy Carter
10. Peter Sellers

84. MORE STONE STUMPERS

1. Identify the Hank Snow song recorded by the Rolling Stones.

2. Who is the chairman of Atlantic Records?

3. What is the flip side of Mick Jagger's single "Memo from Turner"?

4. In October 1978, Keith Richard was ordered by a judge in Canada to give a benefit performance for The Canadian National Institute for the ———.

5. Who began the Stones fan club in England and ran it for years?

6. What is the name of Keith's mansion?

7. Mick Jagger was the best man at the wedding for what noted photographer?

8. Identify the member of English parliament who befriended Mick.

9. Name the book that inspired the Stones' song "Sympathy for the Devil."

10. ——— Poiter was once linked with Brian Jones. In 1978, the Stones made a guest appearance on the American TV satirical show ——— *Night Live.*

THE FILMS OF THE ROLLING STONES (And a Sound-track Album)

85. THE T.A.M.I. SHOW

1. What do the initials T.A.M.I. stand for?

2. Give the two alternate titles of this movie.

3. The T.A.M.I. Awards ceremonies were held at the Civic Auditorium located in what city and filmed via ———.

4. Identify the five songs the Rolling Stones sang in addition to joining in on the closing jam.

These other entertainers appeared with the Rolling Stones on *The T.A.M.I. Show* in 1964. Answer true or false after each act.

5. Jan and Dean

6. The Supremes

7. The Beatles

8. Lesley Gore

9. The Dave Clark Five

10. The Beach Boys

86. CHARLIE IS MY DARLING

1. Who inspired the title of the film?
2. The movie takes place on location in what country?
3. Name the two cities in which the filming took place.
4. In what year was it made?
5. How many days of the Stones' tour are covered?
6. Name the nonmember of the Rolling Stones who receives screen credit for writing songs and incidental music along with Mick Jagger and Keith Richard.
7. Who directed the film? Name the other movie with the Rolling Stones that he also directed.
8. Identify the production company.
9. The movie provides a *cinéma* ——— report of the Stones on tour.
10. What is the running time of the movie?

87. TONITE LET'S ALL MAKE LOVE IN LONDON—The Film

In this movie, the Stones are featured along with the following cast of real-life characters. Match them to their occupations.

1. Allen Ginsberg	a. Pop singer
2. Edna O'Brien	b. Actress
3. Eric Burdon	c. Model
4. David Hockney	d. Nightclub manager
5. Donyale Luna	e. Novelist
6. Lee Marvin	f. Personal manager/record producer
7. Genevieve	g. Beat poet
8. Andrew Loog Oldham	h. Painter
9. Julie Christie	i. Leader of the Animals
10. Vic Lowndes	j. Actor

88. "TONIGHT LET'S ALL MAKE LOVE IN LONDON"—The Sound-Track Album

1. Identify the Jagger/Richard song Chris Farlowe sings.

The following artists are also heard on the sound-track album. Answer true or false after each name.

2. Small Faces

3. Twice As Much

4. Manfred Mann

5. The Marquis of Kensington

6. Freddie and the Dreamers

7. Vashti

8. The Who

9. Lulu

10. Pink Floyd

89. SYMPATHY FOR THE DEVIL

1. The other version of this film is known by what title?

2. Name the character played by Anne Wiazemski.

3. Although the film was made in 1968, it was not released until what year?

4. Identify the Rolling Stones album on which the song "Sympathy for the Devil" first appeared.

5. This album was produced by Jimmy ———.

6. Who directed the movie?

7. Name the co-producer responsible for the changes and additions in his version of the film.

8. Passages are recited from the works of ——— Cleaver.

9. Much of the action takes place in a junkyard full of used ———.

10. The candid view of the Stones working together in *Sympathy for the Devil* is compared to that of the Beatles in what movie?

90. GIMME SHELTER

1. *Gimme Shelter* shows the Rolling Stones on the latter part of their American tour in what year?

2. Name the area where the Rolling Stones were filmed performing in New York City.

3. Ike and Tina ——— appeared on the bill with the Stones at this New York appearance.

4. The Rolling Stones' free concert in California was held at the Altamont ———.

5. Identify the motorcycle club hired to maintain security at Altamont.

6. Payment to this security force amounted to five hundred dollars' worth of ———.

7. What was the name of the young man whose fatal stabbing at Altamont was caught on camera?

8. Name the member of Jefferson Airplane who was injured during the Altamont concert.

9. The Rolling Stones fled Altamont by ———.

10. Altamont was originally planned as the Stones' answer to what East Coast concert movie?

91. ZABRISKIE POINT

1. Name the Rolling Stones song performed by the group on the sound track of *Zabriskie Point*. Who directed the film?

2. Fill in the last names of the actors whose first names are the same as those of the characters they portrayed.

   Daria ———
   Mark ———

3. In real life, Daria was married briefly to which star of *Easy Rider*? Mark met death in a prison mishap after being jailed originally on what charges?

In addition to the Rolling Stone music, *Zabriskie Point* features music by the following groups. Answer true or false after the name of each group.

4. Pink Floyd

5. The Byrds

6. Kaleidoscope

7. The Grateful Dead

8. Peter, Paul, and Mary

9. The Youngbloods

10. The Cyrkle

92. LADIES AND GENTLEMEN, THE ROLLING STONES

1. This rock documentary is known as a ———.
2. In what year was the picture released?
3. Who served as executive producer?
4. The executive producer also functioned as head of what record company?
5. *Ladies and Gentlemen, The Rolling Stones* is a self-proclaimed "film ———" rather than a "concert ———."
6. Who directed the picture?
7. The movie features how many songs recorded by the Stones in Fort Worth, Texas, during one of their American tours?
8. What was the exact date of the recording session?
9. Identify the film's tour production-manager.
10. The tour production-manager was formerly on the staff of ——— East.

THE FILMS OF MICK JAGGER (And Two Movie Albums)

93. INVOCATION OF MY DEMON BROTHER

1. What was the original title of the film?

2. Roll those credits: Mick Jagger was responsible for the movie's music and ———.

3. Who wrote the script and also appears as Magus?

4. One of the characters portrayed is His Satanic Majesty. Give the full title of the Rolling Stones' "Satanic" album.

5. In what year was this album released?

6. American soldiers are shown leaping from helicopters in what country in the film?
7. Some scenes originally shot for ——— *Rising* are reworked here.

8. What ceremonial ritual is performed?

9. Brother and sister of The ——— are featured characters.

10. Name the production company responsible for the picture.

94. *NED KELLY*—The Film

1. Name Mick's real-life girl friend at the time, who was originally set to play his sister.

2. What is the first name of Mick's brother in the film?

3. Who directed the picture?

4. Born in Ireland, the Kellys were deported to what country?

5. Ned and his gang ambush a ——— train.

6. Name the distributor of the film, whose record division also released a movie-related album.

7. In the title role of Ned Kelly, how does Mick meet his death?

8. Where did Ned want to establish a free republic?

9. How old was Ned at the time of his death?

10. What were Ned's last words before dying?

95. "NED KELLY"—
The Original Motion Picture Score Album

1. Who wrote the words and music for the soundtrack of "Ned Kelly"? This composer also wrote "A Boy Named ———" for Johnny Cash.

2. Name the country and western star who sings the title tune.

3. This C & W singer showed his versatility by playing bass as a member of the ——— on Buddy Holly's last tour.

4. Identify the song Mick Jagger sings on the album.

5. Name the two other performers featured on the album.

The following songs are from the movie. Answer true or false after each title.

6. "Stoney Cold Heart"

7. "Hey Ned"

8. "Pleasures of a Tuesday Afternoon"

9. "The Kellys Keep Comin' "

10. "Blame It on the Kellys"

96. *PERFORMANCE*—The Films

1. Name the retired rock star portrayed by Mick Jagger.

2. The gangland boss is named Harry ———.

3. *Performance* was filmed in 1968. In what year was it finally released?

4. Mick lives in a mansion at Notting ——— Gate in the movie.

5. Give the names of his two female roommates.

6. Identify the French actress who portrays one of the roommates.

7. What is the name of the actor who is cast as Chas Devlin?

8. Chas pretends he is an unemployed ———.

9. To avoid identification, Chas has dyed his hair what color?

10. Name the film's two directors.

97. "PERFORMANCE"— The Original Sound-Track Album

1. Who sings the title tune?

2. Name the singer/songwriter who served as musical director.

3. Indicate the song this musical director performs. Aside from the movie, he was responsible for the controversial hit "——— People."

4. Give the title of the song Mick Jagger sings.

5. Who wrote this movie song performed by Mick?

6. Identify the man who arranged and produced the sound track in addition to composing most of the score. Name the earlier film with the Rolling Stones in which he served as musical director.

7. Ry Cooder plays featured solos on guitar and ———.

8. One of the songs is performed by the ——— Poets.

9. Identify the folksinger who performs the vocal on "Dyed, Dead, Red" as well as a mouth ——— solo.

10. "Turner's Murder" is sung by what group?

98. MICHIAL KOHLOSS— DER REBELL

1. The story is set in the ———th century.
2. Keith portrays ——— Man.
3. Who is cast as Katrina?
4. The plot concerns an uprising of ———.
5. Who was the revolt against?
6. Name the country in which the action takes place.
7. In what year was the picture released?
8. Who served as producer?
9. This producer's wife won an Academy Award in 1975 for Best Actress. Identify her.
10. What was the title of the movie for which she captured top acting honors?

THE FILM OF BRIAN JONES

99. A DEGREE OF MURDER

1. The film was made in West ———.

2. What is the foreign title?

3. Name the American company that released the film.

4. In addition to composing the movie sound track, Brian received screen credit for ——— and producing it.

5. Give the first name of the character Anita Pallenberg portrays.

6. Anita is cast as a ———.

7. In the movie, Anita accidentally ——— her former boyfriend to death.

8. Ads for the film claimed, "Men Couldn't ——— Her!"

9. This picture takes place in what city?

10. In what year was the movie released?

ANSWERS

QUIZ 1

1. Blue
2. Taylor
3. Pretty
4. "Reelin' and Rockin' "
   "Bright Lights, Big City"
   "La Bamba"
   "Around and Around"
5. Brian Jones
6. Six
7. Chapman
8. Wetherby; amp
9. Edith
10. Jazz

QUIZ 2

1. Chris; Peggy Lee
2. Incorporated
3. Ealing
4. Brian Jones and Charlie Watts
5. Manfred
6. 1962
7. Marquee
8. *Disc*
9. Ginger; Cream and Blind Faith
10. British

QUIZ 3

1. The Marquee
2. July 12, 1962
3. Harold Pendleton
4. *The Richmond and Twickenham Times*; April 13, 1963
5. Decca
6. Rowe
7. London
8. June 7, 1963
9. *Thank Your Lucky Stars*
10. "England's Newest Hit Makers—The Rolling Stones"; May 1964

QUIZ 4

1. Loog
2. Sandy Beach and Chancery Laine
3. Easton
4. The Beatles
5. Crawdaddy
6. Gomelsky
7. Impact
8. "Come On"; "I Want to Be Loved"
9. Olympic; Savage
10. "I'd Rather Be with the Boys"

QUIZ 5

1. One
2. 66
3. 19
4. 505
5. 2000
6. 2120
7. 2000
8. Five
9. 5
10. 100

QUIZ 6

1. Michael
2. Philip
3. July 26, 1943
4. Leo
5. Whirlwind
6. Eva and Joe
7. Physical
8. Blue
9. Maypole; Keith Richard
10. Chrissie

QUIZ 7

1. Rooster
2. Hog
3. Spider
4. Monkey
5. Dog
6. Beast
7. Horses
8. Bee
9. Cat
10. Monkey

QUIZ 8

1. Lewis
2. Cheltenham
3. February 28, 1942
4. Pisces
5. Buster
6. Ramrods
7. Louisa and Lewis
8. Barbara
9. Donovan
10. Jaujouka; Morocco

QUIZ 9

1. e
2. h
3. d
4. g
5. b
6. i
7. a
8. j
9. c
10. f

QUIZ 10

1. Richards
2. December 18, 1943
3. Sagittarius
4. Sidcup
5. Valerie
6. Brian Jones
7. Marlon
8. "Dandelion"
9. Teeth
10. Toronto

QUIZ 11

1. True
2. False
3. False
4. True
5. False
6. True
7. True
8. False
9. True
10. False

QUIZ 12

1. Perks
2. 1936
3. Scorpio
4. Four
5. The Royal Air Force
6. Diane
7. Stephen
8. Astrid
9. Cliftons
10. "Monkey Grip" and "Stone Alone"

QUIZ 13

1. Rain
2. Satisfied
3. Satisfaction
4. Alright
5. Fire
6. Feeling
7. Found
8. Waiting
9. Gun
10. Why

QUIZ 14

1. Robert
2. June 2, 1941
3. Gemini
4. Harrow
5. Hobson
6. Shirley
7. Serafina
8. "Ode to a High-Flying Bird"
9. People
10. Sheepdog

QUIZ 15

1. Each
2. Last
3. Lonely
4. Bad
5. Papers
6. Side
7. Rambler
8. Wasting
9. Spend
10. Out

QUIZ 16

1. Stew
2. Sixth
3. Rolled
4. Bricklayer's
5. True
6. Maracas
7. Road
8. ICI
9. "Stoned"
10. True

QUIZ 17

A. The Lords Taverners National Playing Fields Association

1. h.
2. d
3. i
4. a
5. g
6. j
7. b
8. e
9. c
10. f

QUIZ 18

1. Dunbar
2. Nicholas
3. Chrissie Shrimpton
4. The Indica
5. John Lennon
6. "As Tears Go By"
7. "Greensleeves"
8. 1964; Andrew Oldham
9. *Rock 'n' Roll Circus*
10. Fur

QUIZ 19

1. False
2. True
3. True
4. True
5. False
6. True
7. False
8. True
9. True
10. False

QUIZ 20

1. Sid Bernstein
2. Allen Klein
3. George Harrison
4. John Lennon and Paul McCartney
5. Love
6. John Lennon; *Town & Country*
7. "Fly"
8. Rich
9. Spector; Johns
10. Mick Jagger and Marianne Faithfull

QUIZ 21

1. Saturday
2. Gear
   Twelve
3. Pops
4. Steady
5. Lucky
6. Jury
7. Sunday
8. Eamonn
9. Park
10. Grey

QUIZ 22

1. Howlin' Wolf and Sam Cooke
2. False
3. True
4. False
5. False
6. True
7. False
8. True
9. True
10. False

QUIZ 23

1. Mother
2. Lennear
3. Hot
4. "The Devil Is My Name"
5. Lurch
6. George Sherlock
7. "Sticky Fingers"
8. Requires
9. Cosmic
10. Black

QUIZ 24

1. January 6, 1964
2. Granada
3. The Ronettes
4. Phil Spector
5. Wilde
6. False
7. True
8. True
9. False
10. True

QUIZ 25

1. Heatherton
2. Taylor
3. Lollobrigida
4. Crawford
5. Garland
6. Mansfield
7. Bardot
8. Monroe
9. Minelli
10. Majors

QUIZ 26

1. False
2. False
3. True
4. False
5. False
6. False
7. True
8. False
9. True
10. False

QUIZ 27

1. June 1964
2. Nose
3. Foreheads; eyebrows
4. "I Just Want to Make Love to You" and "Not Fade Away"
5. The Beatles
6. Father; kill
7. Jerry Lewis
8. Rat
9. Desi
10. Paul; Olivia Hussey; Dorothy Hamill

QUIZ 28

1. June 8, 1969
2. Cotchford
3. *Pooh*
4. At the bottom of his swimming pool
5. Life
6. Misadventure
7. Twenty-seven
8. Harshly
9. "Through the Past, Darkly (Big Hits, Volume 2)"
10. "A Normal Day for Brian, the Man Who Died Every Day"

QUIZ 29

1. Caveman
2. "Don't Look Back"
3. Bush
4. Mick Jagger and Keith Richard
5. The Wailers
6. "Little by Little"
7. The Coasters
8. Gene Pitney
9. Proby
10. "Not Fade Away"

QUIZ 30

1. 1964
2. 1964
3. 1965
4. 1965
5. 1966
6. 1969
7. 1972
8. 1973
9. 1975
10. 1978

QUIZ 31

1. True
2. False
3. True
4. False
5. True
6. True
7. False
8. True
9. False
10. False

QUIZ 32

1. July 5, 1969
2. Hyde
3. 500
4. Shelley
5. *Adonais*
6. Butterflies
7. Crimson
8. Ear
9. Battered
10. New

QUIZ 33

1. True
2. True
3. False
4. True
5. False
6. True
7. False
8. True
9. True
10. False

QUIZ 34

1. June 13, 1969
2. Brian Jones
3. January 17, 1948
4. Capricorn
5. Engraver
6. Afro
7. 1969
8. Five
9. 1974
10. Ron Wood

QUIZ 35

1. 1967
2. English
3. "Dandelion"
4. Whitehead
5. *Wilde*
6. Oscar Wilde
7. Queensbury
8. Marianne Faithfull
9. Bosie
10. *Charlie Is My Darling* and *Tonite Let's All Make Love in London*

QUIZ 36

1. Television
2. December 1968
3. The Robert Frosset Circus
4. Ringmaster
5. Witch
6. Ivry Gitlis
7. *Magical Mystery Tour*
8. *Let It Be*
9. Geraldine Fitzgerald
10. "Something Better"

QUIZ 37

1. d
2. h
3. f
4. j
5. g
6. c
7. i
8. b
9. e
10. a

QUIZ 38

1. Got
2. Confessin'
3. Ventilator
4. Angel
5. Paint
6. Grey
7. Black
8. Jam
9. Yer
10. Schoolboy

QUIZ 39

1. *Hollywood Palace*
2. October 25, 1964
3. Never
4. May 2, 1965
5. Teen-agers; "Let's Spend Some Time Together"
6. The Dave Clark Five
7. Scouts
8. The day before his broadcast
9. Shocked
10. Seventeen

QUIZ 40

1. Bianca Perez Morena de Macias
2. Bianca Rosa Perez-Mora
3. Paris
4. Eddie Barclay
5. Caine
6. Nicaragua
7. Halston
8. Walking
9. Gerald Ford
10. *Trick or Treat*; dirty

QUIZ 41

1. True
2. False
3. True
4. True
5. False
6. True
7. False
8. False
9. True
10. True

QUIZ 42

1. May 12, 1971
2. St. Tropez
3. Nathalie Delon and Roger Vadim
4. Byblos
5. The Chapel of St. Anne
6. Baud
7. Lichfield
8. *Love Story*
9. Catholicism
10. Arts

QUIZ 43

1. d
2. c
3. a
4. f
5. a
6. b
7. a
8. e
9. b
10. a

QUIZ 44

1. True
2. False
3. True
4. False
5. True
6. True
7. True
8. False
9. True
10. False

QUIZ 45

1. Soup
2. Gumbo
3. Salt
4. Apple
5. Peanut
6. Bread
7. Crow
8. Wine
9. Meat
10. Whiskey

QUIZ 46

1. f
2. d
3. a
4. g
5. b
6. a
7. d
8. c
9. e
10. d

QUIZ 47

1. No
2. Jesse
3. October 21, 1971
4. Libra
5. Belvedere
6. Paris
7. Champagne
8. Photographed
9. No
10. Fantastic

QUIZ 48

1. Home
2. My
   Stupid
   Factory
3. Parachute
4. Helper
5. Crazy
6. Tonk
7. Back
8. Dance
9. Some
10. Shadow

QUIZ 49

1. McKinley Morganfield
2. April 4, 1915
3. Rollin'
4. Chess
5. 1964
6. Chicago
7. Chuck Berry and Willie Dixon
8. July 1968
9. The Quiet Knight; Chicago
10. Bill Wyman

QUIZ 50

1. Green
2. Blue
3. $6.99; $7.99; $8.99; $9.99
4. Ball
5. Raquel
6. Fredericks
7. "Just My Imagination (Running Away with Me)"
8. Brassieres
9. Paris
10. Ian McLagan, electric piano
    Mel Collins, sax
    Sugar Blue, harp

QUIZ 51

1. Jack
2. Much
3. Under
4. Mannish
5. D
6. Fighting
7. Beethoven
8. Johnny
9. Turner
10. Wanna

QUIZ 52

1. Slash; Allright
2. End
3. Glyn
4. False
5. True
6. True
7. False
8. True
9. False
10. True

QUIZ 53

1. Brown
2. Silver
3. White
4. Whiter
5. Orange
6. Black
7. Yellow
8. Silver
9. Green
10. Gold

QUIZ 54

1. Mocambo
2. Toronto
3. Sixth
4. Prime
5. 29
6. Three
7. Justin, Sasha, and Michel
8. *Kings and Desperate Men*
9. Patrick McGoohan
10. Sussex

QUIZ 55

1. Susie
2. Jane
3. Amanda
4. Suzie
5. Queenie
6. Virginia
7. Ruby
8. Fanny
9. Delilah
10. Mae

QUIZ 56

1. False
2. True
3. False
4. False
5. True
6. False
7. True
8. False
9. True
10. False

QUIZ 57

1. Five
2. Dartford
3. No
4. 1973
5. John Uribe
6. Back-up vocal
7. Earl
8. Foghat
9. Ekland
10. Sellers; Rod

QUIZ 58

1. Heart
2. Fingerprint
3. Thumb
4. Fingers
5. Heart
6. Hips
7. Hand
8. Eyes
9. Mind
10. Heads

QUIZ 59

1. d
2. h
3. f
4. j
5. g
6. c
7. i
8. b
9. a
10. e

QUIZ 60

1. Tonight
2. Strong
3. Cup
4. Make
5. Vain
6. Long
7. Hide
8. You
9. Somebody
10. Much

QUIZ 61

1. Art
2. Keith Richard and Andrew Oldham
3. Immediate Records
4. Tony Calder
5. True
6. False
7. True
8. True
9. False
10. True

QUIZ 62

1. Woody
2. June 1, 1947
3. Gemini
4. Beck
5. Faces
6. "I've Got My Own Album to Do"
7. Mick Jagger, Keith Richard, Mick Taylor
8. 1974
9. "Now Look"
10. 1975

QUIZ 63

1. i
2. d
3. g
4. b
5. j
6. e
7. a
8. f
9. h
10. c

QUIZ 64

1. False
2. True
3. True
4. False
5. True
6. False
7. True
8. False
9. True
10. True

QUIZ 65

1. 1972 and 1975
2. "That's the Way God Planned It" and "Encouraging Words"
3. "Sgt. Pepper's Lonely Hearts Club Band"
4. "Get Back"
5. Bangla
6. A&M Records
7. Organ
8. Electric
9. George Harrison
10. Nothing

QUIZ 66

1. False
2. True
3. True
4. False
5. False
6. True
7. False
8. True
9. False
10. False

QUIZ 67

1. Bryan Ferry; "Sympathy for the Devil"
2. Fay
3. Terry Jay
4. Texas
5. Paris
6. Three
7. Tall
8. *Marathon Man*
9. Gerri
10. Diamond

QUIZ 68

1. Mick Jagger, Bill Wyman, and Charlie Watts
2. 1972
3. Mick Jagger
4. "Woof Woof"
5. Cooder
6. *Performance*
7. Boudoir
8. Edwards
9. Ry
10. Highland

QUIZ 69

1. e
2. i
3. g
4. b
5. h
6. j
7. c
8. a
9. f
10. d

QUIZ 70

1. Wrestling
2. Repairs
3. Encores
4. The Cockroaches
5. McLagen
6. Mac
7. John Fitzgerald Kennedy
8. Fox
9. Warner
10. Palladium

QUIZ 71

1. Harmony
2. "His Friends Are More Than Fond of Robin"
3. Warren Beatty
4. Elektra
5. 1972
6. Richard Perry
7. "No Secrets" and "The Best of Carly Simon"
8. Taylor
9. Sarah and Benjamin
10. Joanna

QUIZ 72

1. True
2. True
3. False
4. True
5. False
6. False
7. True
8. True
9. False
10. True

QUIZ 73

1. 1971
2. Chester Burnett
3. Ian Stewart
4. Bill Wyman and Charlie Watts
5. Cow
6. Winwood
7. Eric Clapton; Blind
8. Harmonica
9. Ringo Starr
10. January 10, 1976

QUIZ 74

1. Jungle
2. Thirty-three
3. Genya Ravan; Ten Wheel Drive
4. Greatest
5. Marie Laurie; Maurice Gibb, the Bee Gees
6. Wonder; Steveland Morris
7. Kris Kristofferson; *Ned Kelly*
8. Perrin
9. Ollie
10. Pink; punk

QUIZ 75

1. Doncha
2. Rock
3. Imagination
4. Live
5. Lie
6. Catch
7. Cry
8. Let
9. Tell
10. Need

QUIZ 76

1. "Tumbling Dice"
2. False
3. True
4. True
5. False
6. True
7. False
8. False
9. True
10. False

QUIZ 77

1. "Paint It Black"
2. The Animals
3. Dead
4. "Lady Jane" and "Ruby Tuesday"
5. Minnie Ripperton
6. "Sympathy for the Devil"
7. David Clayton-Thomas
8. Purple
9. "Under My Thumb"
10. "(I Can't Get No) Satisfaction"

QUIZ 78

1. False
2. False
3. True
4. False
5. True
6. True
7. False
8. True
9. False
10. True

QUIZ 79

1. Karis
2. November 4, 1970
3. $17
4. 2
5. Mary's
6. Scorpio
7. *Hair*
8. *Othello*
9. Fuzzy Wuzzy
10. California

QUIZ 80

1. "Sticky Fingers"
2. 1971
3. "Brown Sugar"
4. "Let It Rock"
5. Marshall; McGrath
6. "Ladies and Gentlemen, the Rolling Stones"
7. Atlantic
8. Tongue
9. Andy Warhol
10. Bill Wyman

QUIZ 81

1. d
2. e
3. a
4. b
5. d
6. c
7. a
8. e
9. d
10. a

QUIZ 82

1. True
2. True
3. False
4. True
5. False
6. True
7. True
8. True
9. False
10. True

QUIZ 83

1. True
2. False
3. False
4. True
5. True
6. True
7. False
8. True
9. False
10. True

QUIZ 84

1. "I'm Movin' On"
2. Ahmet Ertegun
3. "Natural Magic"
4. Blind
5. Shirley Arnold
6. Redlands
7. David Bailey
8. Tom Driberg
9. *The Master and Margarita*
10. Suki; *Saturday*

QUIZ 85

1. *Teenage Music International*
2. *Teenage Command Performance* and *Gather No Moss*
3. Santa Monica; Electrovision
4. "Around and Around," "Off the Hook," "Time Is on My Side," "It's All over Now," and "It's Alright"
5. True
6. True
7. False
8. True
9. False
10. True

QUIZ 86

1. Charlie Watts
2. Ireland
3. Dublin and Belfast
4. 1965
5. Two
6. Andrew Loog Oldham
7. Peter Whitehead; "Tonite Let's All Make Love In London"
8. Lorrimer Films
9. *Vérité*
10. One hour

QUIZ 87

1. g
2. e
3. i
4. h
5. c
6. j
7. a
8. f
9. b
10. d

QUIZ 88

1. "Paint It Black"
2. True
3. True
4. False
5. True
6. False
7. True
8. False
9. False
10. True

QUIZ 89

1. *1+1*
2. Eve Democracy
3. 1970
4. "Beggars Banquet"
5. Miller
6. Jean-Luc Godard
7. Iain Quarrier
8. Eldridge
9. Cars
10. *Let It Be*

QUIZ 90

1. 1969
2. Madison Square Garden
3. Turner
4. Speedway
5. Hell's Angels
6. Beer
7. Meredith Hunter
8. Marty Balin
9. Helicopter
10. *Woodstock*

QUIZ 91

1. "You Got the Silver"; Michaelangelo Antonioni
2. Halprin
   Frechette
3. Dennis Hopper; bank robbery
4. True
5. False
6. True
7. True
8. False
9. True
10. False

QUIZ 92

1. Rockumentary
2. 1974
3. Marshall Chess
4. Rolling Stones Records
5. Concert; Film
6. Rollin Binzar
7. Fifteen
8. June 24, 1972
9. Chip Monck
10. Fillmore

QUIZ 93

1. *ZAP*
2. Sound
3. Kenneth Anger
4. "Their Satanic Majesties Request"
5. 1967
6. Vietnam
7. *Lucifer*
8. Magick
9. Rainbow
10. Puck Films

QUIZ 94

1. Marianne Faithfull
2. Dan
3. Tony Richardson
4. Australia
5. Police
6. United Artists
7. By hanging
8. In Victoria
9. Twenty-five
10. "Such is life"

QUIZ 95

1. Shel Silverstein; Sue
2. Waylon Jennings
3. Crickets
4. "The Wild Colonial Boy"
5. Kris Kristofferson and Tom Ghent
6. False
7. True
8. False
9. True
10. True

QUIZ 96

1. Turner
2. Flowers
3. 1970
4. Hill
5. Pherber and Lucy
6. Michele Breton
7. James Fox
8. Juggler
9. Red
10. Donald Cammell and Nicolas Roeg

QUIZ 97

1. Merry Clayton
2. Randy Newman
3. "Gone Dead Train"; Short
4. "Memo from Turner"
5. Mick Jagger and Keith Richard
6. Jack Nitzsche; *The T.A.M.I. Show*
7. Dulcimer
8. Last
9. Buffy Sainte-Marie; Bow
10. The Merry Clayton Singers

QUIZ 98

1. Sixteen
2. Nagel's
3. Anita Pallenberg
4. Peasants
5. A landowner
6. Germany
7. 1969
8. Jerry Bick
9. Louise Fletcher
10. *One Flew over the Cuckoo's Nest*

QUIZ 99

1. Germany
2. *Mord und Totschlag*
3. Universal
4. Arranging
5. Marie
6. Waitress
7. Shoots
8. Own
9. Munich
10. 1966

STONES PHOTO QUIZ

1. Silver
2. "I Wanna Be Your Man"
3. Astor
4. Phelge; downtown L.A.
5. "Love You Live"
6. Charlie Watts
7. Jim Morrison; the Doors
8. John Mayall's Blues Breakers
9. Ned Kelly
10. Stargroves
11. Anita Pallenberg; Keith Richard; *Candy*
12. Liver; blubber
13. Glimmer
14. David and Albert Maysles; Charlotte Zwerin
15. The London School of Economics
16. 8:36